Flip

"How to give a 2nd chance to people, situations, and yourself"

Turning Irritation Into Opportunities

SADAF TAUQIR

Flip
Copyright © 2020 Sadaf Tauqir
First published in 2020

Paperback: 978-1-922456-12-0
Ebook: 978-1-922456-13-7

All rights reserved. No part of this book may be reproduced, stored in a retrieval system, or transmitted by any means (electronic, mechanical, photocopying, recording, or otherwise) without written permission from the author.

Because of the dynamic nature of the Internet, any web addresses or links contained in this book may have changed since publication and may no longer be valid. The information in this book is based on the author's experiences and opinions. The views expressed in this book are solely those of the author and do not necessarily reflect the views of the publisher; the publisher hereby disclaims any responsibility for them.

The author of this book does not dispense any form of medical, legal, financial, or technical advice either directly or indirectly. The intent of the author is solely to provide information of a general nature to help you in your quest for personal development and growth. In the event you use any of the information in this book, the author and the publisher assume no responsibility for your actions. If any form of expert assistance is required, the services of a competent professional should be sought.

Publishing information
Publishing, design, and production facilitated by Passionpreneur Publishing,
A division of Passionpreneur Organization Pty Ltd, ABN: 48640637529

www.PassionpreneurPublishing.com
Melbourne, VIC | Australia

TABLE OF CONTENTS

1	Introduction	1
2	Do You Like Roller Coasters?	15
3	Warm-Up	23
4	2nd Chance to People	27
5	2nd Chance to Circumstance	37
6	2nd Chance to Yourself	53
7	Mindset Matters	61
8	"Sometimes Building a New Bridge Is a Lot of Work Compared to Fixing the Old One"	77
9	Conclusion	87
	Disclaimer	91

1

INTRODUCTION

We are here in this world with so many other people. We like some of them and we don't like others, or should I say, we don't like most of them. Don't you just wish that you had a remote control for other human beings so you could control them? Ok, given a choice, which button would you like to use the most? Once I asked the same question in an elevated pitch in front of 60 people, and they all said, given a choice, if we had a remote control for other people, we will use the button "STOP." I used to think the same until I realised that it is not only them we would like to "STOP" but we can also use the same button for ourselves sometimes:

- Press "STOP" to our prejudgmental thoughts and assumptions.
- Press "STOP" to all our burdening emotional baggage.
- Press "STOP" to unnecessary resistance to nature.
- Press "STOP" to our closed mindset.

- Press "STOP" to unnecessary irritation towards other people.

"STOP" above all and try to "FLIP" the scenario in a healthy direction.

We are easily irritated by everything and anything. Mostly, it happens when we are in a bad mood. I would like you to pause for a minute, **FLIP**, and ask yourself:

"How often are you in a bad mood?"

Well, you can say, "I am in a bad mood because of people around me."

I can ask another question.

"What if it is the other way around; for example, you are in a bad mood and that's why you are irritated by so many people?"

Or

"You are irritated by one person and you just let that irritation pass on to others?"

This book serves as your reflection journal. It contains a number of questions and self-talk dialogues. What I want from you is to be honest and open-minded when you answer them. You don't have any reason to be shy here; try to be generous with your thoughts. I will help you explore your triggers, and it will give you the capabilities to manage yourself and other people effectively. The new trend is that people are very intolerant towards other people. We don't realise it on this "Irritation Journey"—how much hate we create and how many opportunities we miss. Let us turn these irritations into opportunities. The human race has seen so much in terms of experiences and experiments that they should be enough to teach us what works in life and what doesn't. We have a massive amount of information around us and still it doesn't help us. This is a worrisome situation. Let us join hands to help ourselves, so that together we can help others. Wait! It doesn't stop here. When we help others, we actually gain a lot in return. That last stretch involving "gain a lot" is the agenda of this book.

We will start our journey of "How to give a 2nd chance to people, situations, and yourself." I have set a pace where you will peel your beliefs like an onion. ☺

This lifestyle of "2nd chance" has prerequisites:

1. Heal yourself.
2. Find your passion.

When the two prerequisites are met, you can start working on your relationships.

I had a chance to interview this beautiful soul, Corry McDonald, for my book. She is a creative healer and author of the book titled *Creating Healing: How Crayons and Childlike Curiosity Can Activate the Creative Intelligence You Are*. She integrates three key modalities that helped to heal her subconscious conditioning—Transpersonal Art Therapy, Energy Healing, and Heart Speak. Her work is all about healing. This game-changing phenomenon of 2nd chances starts with healing yourself. A "hurt" you will be "hurting" others. She is a big advocate of healing, forgiving yourself, and growing from it. She shares three suggestions on how you can turn "Irritation into Opportunities":

1. Another person is a projected part of you. This is an opportunity for you to reflect on yourself. Whatever you don't like, it's a hidden message for you. Explore it and outgrow it.
2. When you are with someone, just be present. Don't bring any should'ves and would'ves onto the table.
3. See your OMG (Oh My God) experiences as opportunities. Keep an eye on the process. When nothing triggers you, it means you have grown from that pain.

If you are unable to heal on your own, you can always go to a professional like Corry (www.corrymacdonald.net). Feel free to contact her for your healing needs.

Next is your Passion. First of all, you have to find your passion; to support you in this search. I have interviewed one of the world's top experts on the topic of passion. He believed in passion to the extent that he was named "Mr. Passion" by the late Prof. Tony Buzan, the inventor of mind mapping. Moustafa Hamwi, or Mr. Passion, is also the author of the international best-seller book *Live Passionately*, and he shares insights into what passion is and how to find it.

According to him, passion is "consistently doing what you love, are good at, and is of value to the world."

Passion is purpose; so it is about looking inward to know your calling and then dedicating your life towards pursuing that calling so that the other priorities in your life become less relevant. If you are not pursuing the most passionate life ever, you will simply be in continuous irritation with yourself, and this irritation will project outward at people around you.

So, in order to find your passion and true calling, he suggests you to answer these two key questions:

1. If you have a check for a billion dollars, what will you do with your life?
2. If today is the last day of your life, what will you regret not doing?

This will be a great start to know if you are going in the right direction or not. If your answers to these questions are very far from where you are today, then you might have a clue about the deeper reason for your irritations.

Another trick I learned from Moustafa to overcome this irritation was to "find the blessings" in these irritations.

Step 1: Write the answers to the first two questions on one side of a paper.
Step 2: On the opposite side, write things (or people) that are consistently irritating you.
Step 3: Now, find as many connections on how the current irritations are helping you achieve your passions.

When I did this exercise with Moustafa, I noted down my passions: "Learning, family, and self-love." What triggers me in other people is "continuous complaining and unprofessional behaviour." Then I thought about how the "unprofessional attitude of other people" is helping me achieve my passion for "learning."

And how handling people with "continuous complaining" is helping me learn how to handle kids, which is part of my passion regarding "family." With this technique, you can turn your irritations around or actually see them for what they truly are—"blessings."

So simply put, pursuing your passion will guide your energy towards living a fulfilled life, which will surely make you less irritated (with the average stuff) and maybe more irritated towards lack of passion—the good kind of irritation. And if you want to pursue a more passionate life, you can go to www.moustafa.com to watch some of his interviews.

Your passion is what defines you as a person. I have lived in a nuclear set-up with an extended family. I can very confidently say this—that my career saved me from a lot of family and friends chaos. My job was my passion. Yes! I am fulfilling my responsibility, but that adrenaline and feel-good hormone were what I always got from my career. My passion defined me as a person; it made me forget to be part of any family or friends politics. This feeling is normal and so many people are irritated with each other. We see so much hate and rage around us. Sometimes, we are the victim and sometimes we are the reason. In either case, someone is hurting. In some cases, people grow from experiences. They get better with age, but sometimes they don't; any amount of experience is not worth it when we don't open our hearts. It just doesn't happen because we are unconsciously blocking ourselves due to our negative mindset. We always feel that we are the "victim," and not the "reason." Depending on your age, you will perceive things differently. Just be mindful of how things happen around you and what they are teaching you. We are not perfect and neither is anyone else. We have flaws; so do everyone. We cannot judge anyone and they cannot judge us either. If we cannot help anyone, let us not add to their problems. We don't have an exact formula on how to make ourselves and other people happy. But, if I want to give you some simple advice, I would say, *"Don't get irritated by other people.* Try to flip the scenario that gives you opportunities." This is the best you can do for yourself and others.

You might argue that other people are so stupid and annoying. My question to you is: "Are all of them stupid and annoying?" If your answer is "No," I am happy that you are being realistic and you are open to progress and to having better relationships. But, if your answer is "Yes" . . . maybe, then you are the one who is most annoying! #foodforthought!

My success started when I stopped depending on my pre-defined realities based on my experiences. It happened to me by accident and, honestly, it was in times of desperation. I was not planning to find this part of life, but it happened, and I am so pleased. Even if I am not right all the time, at least I am willing to take chances. "Freedom" to take a chance is freedom from the presumptions of the mind. As much as I love being smart, I don't like how our mind manipulates us sometimes. The mind war doesn't stop here. After our mind shows us a picture, it makes sure to collect all the evidence in favour of it; so, we are bound to follow our mind's first impression.

I used to get irritated by people for doing small, silly things. I never realised that there is a world beyond my judgment. If we deserve a 2nd chance in life or from people around us, so do they!

To progress and move forward, we have to give a 2nd chance to so many things. Sometimes, we give chances to other people, we give 2nd chances to situations, and very importantly, we give chances to our own self.

Remember this . . . We give 2nd chances to:

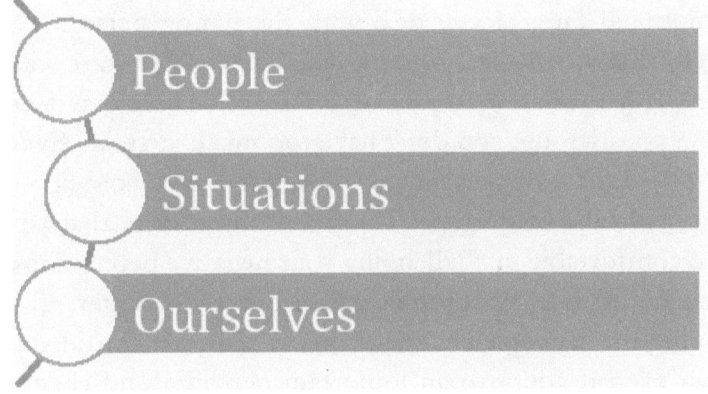

If your ego hurts by being kind and nice, tell yourself that you love excitement, you want to take risks, and that is why you take chances and give chances. Sometimes you may regret it; that is why I propose a structure or a road map that you can navigate. No matter how many videos you watch, podcasts you listen to, and books you read, you can never understand what is on the other side of your perception and mindset until you start looking for it yourself. I understand you are afraid to try and explore, so the best way is to start small. Start with people who do not affect you massively or people whose damage control is easy to manage. Start changing your perception about one person, interact with them, and see how it feels. If it doesn't work, try another one. You need to have at least three to five mini positive experiences before you are actually ready to give anyone a 2nd chance. If you are very hurt for any reason, if you are scared that you will be taken advantage of, if you are worried that you will get into an emotional mess if you deal with the wrong person . . . well, that is why you have to start small. You start with people who are not very close to you and in case that decision goes wrong, you don't have too much at stake. Even if you don't gain anything, you won't lose much either. We will take baby steps. The main objective is that you are comfortable in challenging your negative perceptions, you are ok to let your mind explore otherwise. Later, after giving these people chances, you can gain the confidence that even if you give an important person a 2nd chance in your life, you will still be in control of how you want things to be eventually.

Here are a few questions that might cross your mind.

Why should I try this in the first place?

Answer: Before you answer the above question, ask yourself these questions:

Do other people bother me a lot?

Am I easily annoyed?

Am I happy/satisfied with my relationships?

Is my mind fully aware of all the possibilities and facts about everyone all the time?

What is holding me back from seeing how things work out if I give people another chance?

If you don't have any clear or convincing reply to the above questions, let us flip the story.

What if the person I didn't give a chance to, is the one who has solutions to my problem?

What if that annoying person is a quick solution to the struggles I face in life?

What if I give another person a chance to prove themselves and they exceed my expectations?

I will eventually get what I want but it may be a long process. Otherwise, I will keep on struggling. How do I feel about this?

What will happen if I am open-minded towards all my life experiences?

Now you can answer the first question we asked:

Why should I try this in the first place?

2

DO YOU LIKE ROLLER COASTERS?

Let me give you a metaphor. Do you like roller coasters? If yes, then you get on the ride, go as fast as you can, and still return safe. You trust the maker of that roller coaster. It's the same with this world. Trust the creator, trust who is running the world; we have a system in place. This roller coaster is part of the plan, and you will eventually arrive safe. Well, on the other hand, if you don't like roller coasters, you can skip this metaphor. ☺

If you don't enjoy roller coasters, I have a different metaphor for you. Imagine you have burned your hand slightly on an iron. The next time, you will be careful when touching the iron. Yes, you are hurt, but you will not start wearing wrinkled clothes; you will just be more careful when ironing them. So even if you are hurt, you will not quit. You will just be more careful. You do this with "things," so why not with "people"? Take relatives, for example. You won't throw them out but will still be careful. We are social animals, and I don't see ourselves progressing alone; we need followers to be successful; we need family to take care of us and we take care of them; we need people to buy or run our business. I can give you a million other examples of where we need people.

I know that maybe a lot of people say that staying where you are miserable is wrong. My question is: who is making you miserable—your own perception or the other person? Sometimes, our misery is created by ourselves and we just fall into this trap. My request here is that before you jump to a conclusion, try to get a confirmation that blocking that person from your life is the only solution. Sometimes, just to be happy, we end up being miserable, and we tend to choose a difficult path. I think, after listening to so many self-care motivational videos, we think we are only happy if we are away from whoever tends to disturb our peace. I think this has gone too far and we've ended up being emotionally paranoid. My culture has taught me how to dance in the rain with so many people around me. In my culture, I cannot imagine a strict schedule. I don't have the luxury to get peace whenever I want; I cannot write in my journal or meditate regularly at a set time. I have always had too many people around me. So does this mean that I cannot be successful? I love western research and studies, but sometimes I cannot adopt them as they are. I made changes that suited my situation and it did wonders. I believe that we can be successful with whatever challenges we have. "Other people" are a challenge sometimes, and now we will get better in handling them. A person coming from my collectivist culture cannot work on themselves alone. First, they have to settle their responsibilities and in the middle of all that, they try to find their way. This is exactly what I did. Books out there talk about "me, myself, and I." What if I don't have a choice to be "me, myself, and I"? If I would have been annoyed with everyone and I don't have a choice to leave them, can you imagine how miserable I would have been? If you feel yourself to be in a similar situation, this book will give you the confidence to manage people around you and still be successful.

I believe that we have to explore ourselves, but in some cases you explore yourself by being around other people. You explore yourself differently at different times. You find yourself, whenever you get a chance. I have devised a strategy that can help you attain your higher self. It will happen in a few steps. You have to be mindful of your experiences. You remember, earlier, we talked about how we can give a 2nd chance to **"people, situations, and yourself"?** This is where it all begins. Keep an eye on someone you just misjudged based on your perception. You just have to deal with that person once and you don't have any stakes, even if this negative perception is right. In simpler words, if you don't gain anything from this interaction, you will not lose anything as well. I will share a few examples in upcoming chapters. Before that, let me give you a clear idea of how you will take these risks and how, without losing much, you will become better at it.

We will talk about irritation from other people in **five categories.**

1. **One-time dealing:** These are people who are not close to you; they are not your friends. You probably deal with them once and that is it. For example, in my case, I will put my realtor in that category.
2. **People working under you:** The second type is where you might have to deal with a person on a regular basis, but you have a choice to discontinue your arrangements given the fact that your assumption about them is correct. (I will put my house help in that category; you can put your subordinates in that category.)
3. **Friends:** The third category is friends. You like someone as a friend and you want to be with them. So if you have a bad experience, most likely you will be over cautious with every other friend. We will talk about how can we gracefully move on and give situations a 2nd chance. Here, just be aware of the lessons you learn. Try not to forward that bad experience to anyone else.
4. **Your boss:** The fourth category is someone above you. Once you have experienced a bully boss, the impact can stay for very long. We will talk about how you can rewire yourself to get different results.

5. **Your loved ones:** This is the most challenging category. You love someone and they hurt you. This is terrible, and it's not easy to give such people a 2nd chance. Here we will see how you can remain in the situation and be more productive.

In points 1 and 2, you are giving a 2nd chance to someone you misjudged due to your perception. Points 3 and 4 are tricky ones in terms of relationships. It is hard to go back to the same people with similar feelings in these cases. We have to be realistic, yet we cannot evaluate all the cases using the same parameters. So these are the cases where you will learn from experience and you will give the situations a 2nd chance. This time you will set rules and you will define limits and there is no harm in it. One bully boss shouldn't be the reason for you to quit your job and never go back to a corporate setup. If an opportunity comes, you will evaluate and you will decide what conditions you will apply this time. Your peace is more important. Due to your past experience, you are smarter and more vigilant. In this case, just make sure you are not passing down your negative experiences. Whatever happened to you in those situations, kindly don't replay them with anyone else. Your horrible childhood doesn't mean that you have to be a toxic parent; your messed-up friendship doesn't mean that you hurt someone else; your bully boss doesn't mean that you have to be a horrible boss. If you repeat the same scenario, it means that you are not giving the situations a 2nd chance. You can have the same situation, with new characters, but this time you will lead the story with your rules and wisdom.

Let me share my interview with Navana Kundu here. She is a "multi-therapist coach" and the author of the book *Emotional Mastery*. She has shared some great advice on how to turn "Irritation into Opportunities" from an emotional mastery perspective:

1. Know yourself to know others. Every reality happens twice—once in the mind and the second time outside. So outside, if something or someone is not as per your liking, look inside. You are not against the person, but certain behaviours or thought processes of that person are pointing at your own open wound or pain from the past, which is hiding under the carpet and screaming, "Look at me, I am here too." The other person is only a trigger to look at your own trash within.
2. Do not be a snoozer. Learn from your past mistake and rectify it. Some people keep snoozing their alarm. Make a decision to wake up at the first call.
3. Do not look at the rearview mirror when you want to drive your car forward. Else your car will crash. Most of us are living our past relationships in our present partner.

These are some great bits of advice. Like I said before, to go on this journey, you have to heal and find a passion. We have so many experts on that—you can connect to anyone you like. So, once you are healed and have found your passion, let us start our 2nd chance journey. If you don't trust your judgment and decisions, you will always avoid taking risks. This is what we will practice through this book. We will take this process objectively and slow. We will flip to be successful. I wish you all the best on this beautiful journey.

FIRST STEP:
2nd chance to people: We will start with Step 1, which is the minimum amount of emotional risk. In such cases, you can easily replace options and try and ensure that you are not emotionally vested.

Example:
One-time interactions and people working under you.

SECOND STEP:
2nd chance to situations: This is where you are not ready to give any chance to the same person; this happens and it is ok. Sometimes, bad experiences don't let us be comfortable with the same person. I would suggest you keep this list as short as possible because it is a war between the mind and the heart. Just be mindful of how much damage control you have in this case. We acknowledge the fact that this interaction didn't work out the way you expected, but you do not abandon the circumstances. Here, you give a 2nd chance to the situation. For example, someone's not getting married due to their parents messed-up marriage.

One experience with a bad friend cannot stop you from making friends. One bad boss shouldn't stop you from working for another boss. In this case, you will give the same situation another chance with new characters and new rules.

Example:
Your friends and your boss.

THIRD STEP:
2nd chance to yourself: Step 3 is the most challenging one. Here you are giving yourself another chance. You are being forgiving to yourself and you are growing from the experience.

Example:
Close relationships and family.

3

WARM-UP

If you haven't done this before, let's warm-up. Here you can start your journaling.

Have you noticed that as a human being we are so intolerant towards other people? I have seen many people turning from extroverts to introverts. I agree that with age it becomes difficult to deal with other people, but I feel that it's more of a drama that we enjoy. The drama is of being selective—the drama of not giving a damn about other people, the drama of being your unique self, and the drama of being isolated and thinking that we are the best.

Let us try to do things differently. Imagine you have a negative opinion about someone. Give that person a chance to provide you with evidence to prove you are right or wrong. Maybe the person proves you wrong; you will gain confidence in challenging your mind. I have seen people who were very social and now they avoid people. I know they have become selective about whom they want to meet but on the other hand, I also feel that they miss out on some potential positive connection due to their own assumptions. Our mind enjoys drama, and we keep on feeding it. But, just saying you do not care and shutting all the doors doesn't make you careless. Shutting a door to other people gives us a feeling that we are securing ourselves, but have you ever questioned that maybe whatever reality you have in your mind about the other person is not true?

Let us ask a few more questions and then we will jump into a new chapter.

What do you do when you don't like someone?

What is your criterion to like or dislike someone?

What is your relationship with that someone?

Have you changed over time?

Do you trust that other people also change over time?

Mention one example where you have seen someone change for the better.

26 FLIP

What inspiration do you get from this?

4

2ND CHANCE TO PEOPLE

One-time interaction
Four years back, I was in touch with a realtor for our property. We wanted to give it on rent. I would receive calls and messages now and then. One day, I received a message from a female agent. From the initial message, she sounded a bit annoying. I felt she was asking too many questions. I don't know why, but I felt it was unreasonable at that time. Anyways, as usual, like we have been told to shut down whoever annoys you, I blocked her number. After that, I talked to many agents. Many tenants came for viewing, but somehow things didn't work out. Our house was empty, the mortgage payment was going as usual, and we were now facing financial troubles. I was wondering why things were not working out. What were we doing wrong? So many people came and saw the house. Why didn't we have a single offer

to consider? With all these questions in my mind, I was scrolling through my mobile phone and I saw that female agent's number—the one I'd blocked. Now, when I went through her messages, they didn't seem to be annoying at all. I asked myself why I had blocked her at that time. Anyways, stuck in this rental crisis, I unblocked her. After unblocking her, I thought I should start a conversation. I messaged her, "Hi, how are you? Any update on tenants?" She replied, "Yes, I have a client. Can you arrange a viewing?" I said yes, so we arranged a viewing. The guy came, saw our house, and left. Next day, he made an offer and, within a week, with the help of the same agent, we closed the deal. How insane is this? I went into reflection mode, thinking how I had tried to close the door, but that was actually my only path. I was happy I gave that agent another chance.

Apparently, this is not a big deal, but it definitely gives some insights. It just gave me food for thought on how I can be so judgmental about someone. Let's be honest; most often we ignore the person after judging them. Later, our ego doesn't let us go back to our decision for reflection.

The following three sections in the next three chapters will help in your journey:

1. Self-talk: This is my internal dialogue which I have shared with you.

2. Reflection chair: These are the questions you can ask if you are in a similar situation.
3. Flip: Write down what new feelings and thoughts are emerging. You can say a different side of the same coin.☺

Self-talk

Why didn't I talk to this realtor before? Maybe because I didn't want to . . . Ok that is fine, it happens. But was there any reason? No, no reason. I think it was something in my mind. I reached out to her because I was stuck. I am happy I gave it a chance, it wasn't bad at all. So, I will be open-minded from now on.

Let me use a metaphor to define this situation. It is like we got an unwanted gift (a vase) and without even trying to put it to use, we give it to a friend and somehow, that unwanted gift comes back to us again. Just because I now have the same gift again, I think, "Ok, let me use this." Surprisingly, now, I find a perfect spot for it and it looks amazing. I wouldn't have found that perfect spot if I had put it in storage. In fact, I wouldn't have known if it is wanted or unwanted until I opened it. I never closed my door for gifts, and that is a good thing. So take such "one-time dealing" judgmental experiences as unwanted gifts. You never know how useful it is until you use it. Such interactions are not a burden. You don't gain anything; you will not lose anything. It is extremely safe to give such interactions a "2nd chance." This is the safest zone to challenge your negative judgments. Give it a try and note down how you feel. The options you disapprove still exist in reality. To approach this option with an open mind is a challenge. How can you see beyond your irritation? That is the skill you can work on to begin with. Take this one-time example as a sample test of a bigger medicine; take such small risks towards life. Don't put everything at stake and don't shut down everything. Try to release yourself from being the "slave of your own perceptions."

Reflection chair
Here are some examples to help you:

1. Should I give this person who helped me a 2nd chance? (Yes/No)

If "Yes," I didn't lose anything, I actually gained, and my issue is sorted now.

If "No," ok, I didn't gain anything and I didn't lose anything either. It was just an experience.

2. Am I open to this experiment again? (Yes/No)

If "Yes," cool, I will know more about other people and my own perceptions.

If "No," how will I challenge my perceptions when it comes to the more important people in life?

Flip: New Thoughts and Feelings

It's your turn now. Add your notes here.

People working under you

I will start with my interview with Pegah Gol. She is a career coach and recruitment expert with over a decade of experience in award-winning executive search firms. She collected her experiences of job-hunting in her Amazon #1 best-selling book called *The Formula: The Ultimate Guide to Modern Job Finding*.

In my interview with her, she explained how we can be misled by our judgmental mind and first impressions, which could continue to gather evidence to convince us that our misperception was correct.

Pegah shared an example. Approximately 35 percent of job applicants have been abandoned by recruiters due to the misjudgment of their CVs. She decreased the number of neglected CVs and increased the candidates' placements by giving them the benefit of the doubt and having a quick conversation with them to understand them better before judging them and, surprisingly, she found amazing applicants behind not-so-amazing CVs.

She shared three tips on how we can turn a misjudgment to true understanding:

1. She said we see the world through our judgmental mind; as soon as we remove the judgmental lenses from our eyes, we see everyone as a human being. And, by understanding that we all have the presence of God within, we can see all as one; however, we may not be able to see the similarity due to our ego.
2. If we feel some negative emotions triggered in us due to someone's action or a situation, it is actually a time to reflect on ourselves instead of being annoyed and irritated. Other people can be our mirror. Finding out why we react that way will help us to understand the cause of the triggering in us.
3. When we find a route, then we can heal it. As we heal them, they won't trigger us anymore like before. When you investigate, you will find an answer and it will make sense.

I agree with Pegah and you can look at your own experiences. Everyone has a story to share. It can be any interaction where you can replace your selection. My example is not a big corporate job selection, but just someone I wanted as my house help. A few years back, I was looking for a helper/housemaid in Dubai, since my previous helper had left after five years. My old helper was very kind and helpful, docile, and simple. I was kind of spoiled by her and somehow I had the same criteria when I started to look for a new maid. One maid came through a referral. She fits the apparent criteria, but her work wasn't meeting my needs. Anyways, I tried her for three months and I had to excuse her from the job. I kept looking for another maid. One day, my agency sent me Jane's profile as a house help. I got her number and interviewed her. I was not comfortable with her WhatsApp profile picture. I am sorry, this might sound weird, but I come from a conservative background and if I have to keep someone in the house, I have to be sure that we share the same values. I rejected that maid based on her profile picture and our few initial conversations. I asked the agency to look for another one. They kept looking for someone else, but unfortunately it didn't work out. Now almost a month had passed, and I was still unable to find anyone. That evening, I sat down and started to reevaluate my situation. I asked myself the worst that could happen if I hired her. If she joined me, would I be able to request her to wear some modest clothing? I had the option of letting her go if her lifestyle didn't match our values. I asked myself how long I could wait to find the perfect house help. I was badly stuck because of her picture. She matched every other criterion I had. My situation was desperate as I had a big project coming up and the kids were off from school. Anyways, trying to be positive and careful in a desperate situation, I called her to join. To date, she has been the best. She is the most professional and active house help I've ever had. I ignore her little mistakes and overall, she is not at all what her picture and conversations portrayed.

Self-talk:
Why did I reject her earlier? Just because of her profile picture. I felt she dressed in very revealing clothes. Does it affect her work? Not as such, but I would prefer modest clothing in the house. Ok, so can you tell her this? Of course, I can request her; if she listens, it will be very good and if she doesn't, then we will see what to do. So what is more important—your job or her dressing? My job, of course. Ok, let's call her so you can focus on the things that are more important. Well, she is here now, so how is it going? Well, I didn't have to say anything since she is modestly dressed and is very professional. Bingo, here you go. I am very bad at judging people. I should stop it.

In the above two examples, I got so stuck with the other person's habit or personality or on my own judgment, that I couldn't see beyond. At that moment, they felt big but later on, it didn't feel irritating to me. Sometimes chances come to us and we just take a decision on what we want to believe in. I would have never explored how it felt to be wrong or right. Yes, accepting we are wrong is not easy; many people get stuck with their decisions. Maybe it's the ego, habit, insecurity, or fear that stops us from reevaluating our decisions and changing our beliefs. I abandoned two opportunities due to irritation. Once I sat with an open mind and open heart, it all worked out.

I have seen people suffer when they don't reconsider their decision. Even when my decision was based on a right/wrong list, being open about it and giving it another chance actually helped me. It takes a lot of courage to accept that we can be wrong. We usually take a decision based on our experiences and mindset. At that particular point, the decision we took was right due to the circumstances we were in. Given a very simple situation, with less emotional damage, we didn't pick option A. We were looking for option B and it is perfectly ok... but by any chance, have you ever gone back to the option you rejected? Is there a possibility that maybe you could have gone back to option A and you didn't? What do you think would have happened if you had gone for option A again? Though at that given point, option A was annoying and irritating... still, would you go back to try if that's an opportunity?

Try this out and write down how you feel.

Reflection chair:

Examples:

Am I in a good mood all the time?

Is it possible that I am taking out my irritation on someone else?

I don't judge people but sometimes, unconsciously, it happens. Is it true?

I am comfortable with my own values. Can I instill my values in other people?

Do I have an option if they don't agree? If yes, then I think it is safe to try it out. I can always replace the person and get someone else.

Flip: New Thoughts and Feelings

It's your turn now. Add your notes here!

5

2ND CHANCE TO CIRCUMSTANCE

I will not push you to be generous and forgiving all the time. Sometimes you have to put your foot down because of your own emotional well-being. My point here is that not all relationships need a closed door with a big lock on it. Keep it slow, heal, find passion, and give chances to other people with less emotional risk capacity. If you have done this all, you are justified to shut your door to other people. If you cannot stay in the same situation, leave it, learn from it, come back later with an open mind and kind heart, but when you come back, remember to play by your rules, with new characters. Don't let any bad situation be a reason for negativity, which you will eventually be spilling everywhere.

I am sharing two personal examples:

1. Friends.
2. Bully boss.

Friends:
When we moved to Dubai, I met a few people from my husband's office. Being a stranger in a new country, I was full of excitement and questions and ideas. I had no clue that I was being judged. I came to know from a mutual friend that I should be careful and not be around a particular group of people. At first, I didn't believe the friend, but later I realised that our mutual friend was right. I got bad vibes and I felt very much disrespected. Anyways, after a few confusing incidents, we drifted apart and our friendship ended in a confusing way.

The years have passed, we have made new friends, and our social circle is pretty cool to hang out with. So at the end, I have no regrets, but it taught me how I should deal with people, how to behave when new to a country, and other lessons as well. A person who is new to any experience comes with a different frequency—anything new from motherhood to a new job, a new country, a new relationship, etc. Just understand that the frequency will eventually match if we can draw an emotional boundary and still be supportive. As a supportive person, give them space to adjust. What are your chances of losing anything? Once you are a family person and you have a job, kid, self-care agenda, etc., you have a choice of how much you want your friends to interfere. My first interaction with friends in Dubai taught me that it's ok if I am not aligned with someone, but it is not ok to gang up against a friend for your own psychological comfort.

It is a good idea to define priorities. If you have a family and work, it is a good idea to set boundaries with friends. At least this is how it is done in my part of the world. Mostly, if they are in the same situation as you are, they will understand your point. Just to feel good inside, you don't have to be out and about with anyone and everyone. To be kind to others, you have to be kind to yourself. You cannot just be out there and expect that everything will happen as you desire. If you gain energy from meeting people, just enjoy it the way it is. Don't go into "paralysis by analysis" in friendship. It takes a lot to manage all relationships differently. Define and acknowledge where you will put your spouse, kids, parents, siblings, friends, colleagues, or acquaintances in your attention hierarchy. I have realised with time that not everyone can receive the same amount of effort and attention from you. I think if we can manage this attention, we won't have any reason to hate anyone. In regular circumstances, just check who are you giving your attention to. If you are giving your full attention to everyone, you might go into a wrong emotional battle. The problem is not that the other person is wrong; the issue is that you are drained and you cannot keep up with all the energies around you. It is good to take a break from people if you feel like judging them. In friendship, just try to invest healthy time. If you cannot help anyone, try not to hurt them. I have also learned it late, but when I realised it, I made sure to be mindful around friends. You cannot be a taker or giver all the time. All relationships are a mix of both giver and taker.

Let me give an example of what made me realise that I might be getting angry with people for no reason. If you have kids, you will understand. You know sometimes how much you love your kids and another moment you hate them? These feelings are the same in some instances. Kids don't change as such, but we fall in love with them again, just because we want to. Sometimes the loud TV will annoy me and sometimes it doesn't; sometimes their stupid jokes will bother me or sometimes it will not. Again, I sat on a reflection chair to understand what was going on. I realised that 90 percent of how I react depends on my mood. Kids are just being their true self. This made me think about the world outside my house. Is there a chance that I am annoyed due to my bad day or bad mood?

Self-talk:
Why is my friend so stupid/annoying? Well maybe he/she doesn't know any better. So how is it my fault if he/she is stupid? No, it is not your fault, but do you think maybe you can help him/her? No, I am not sure if I want to sign up for this? Ok hold on . . . if you cannot help him/her can you be just "not rude" to him/her? Well,

yeah, not being rude to him/her won't kill me and with that I will choose some reasonable boundaries so I don't lose my patience with this friend. Ok, yeah, this seems to be reasonable. Later, if I develop trust and he/she asks me clearly about my opinion, I can tell him/her nicely what I think . . . but before that I have to make sure that my friend is actually annoying. It's not just my mood which is filtering all the information. Let's hold my final verdict on stupidity right now.

A few months back, I met a girl named Sara. We met at our friend's place. After some conversation, she mentioned that she had just moved to Dubai. That got my attention. She was full of questions and excitement. Somehow, when she was talking to me, I could only see my ten years younger self in the picture. That moment took me to my past and my first confusing interaction with those friends. I came back to the moment and I tried to help her as much as I could. Our few initial meet-ups were very good. I introduced her to my other group of friends. I tried hard to include her in our weekend plans. I know that a person coming to a new city is unfamiliar with many things. When you are not in your home country, your friends fulfil your social needs. Good friends are a healthy replacement for your family. Sara used to mention how she misses her family, and I could relate to her. Now, after a few weeks of interaction, she would message me with small talk. Her random messages would pop up throughout the day. Honestly, there was a time when I was a bit annoyed at these messages. To me, it seemed like stupid queries. At moments like these, I used to reflect, and I had to remind myself how it was like to be an alien in a new city with so many strangers. My intention to connect with other people was not bad; I was just settling in. After this self-talk, I would go back to Sara's messages and reply to each one of them. For me, I was giving a 2nd chance to an expat who was new to the city and trying to settle in. I cannot tell you how much she respects me now. I didn't do much. I didn't let myself get irritated; I didn't let her take control of my mood; I didn't talk about her naivety—I was just trying not to hurt someone the way I was hurt.

Reflection chair:
Example:
Have you ever thought about what it will be like if you are in your friend's shoes? If you have passed the age or experience of what she/he is going through right now, maybe you know better. You don't have to impose yourself; just be there with your neutral self. I think it's a good idea to understand the other person's situation as if you were there earlier. If you don't have experience of what he/she is saying right now, how can you judge or evaluate them?

Our life scenes are connected. We can rewind and see how we felt and fast forward to anticipate that we cannot be 100 percent sure as to how to respond.

Flip: New Thoughts and Feelings

It's your turn now. Add your notes here!

Bully boss:
We work for money, skill, passion, or a sense of belongingness. Spending a minimum of 40 hours per week in a place and feeling miserable is something no one would want. Honestly, if you ask me, this point is the trickiest one to write. This is such a subjective matter. Unfortunately, sometimes you have to work for that terrible boss. This relationship doesn't come under love, care, or a one-time deal. So, if someone is working under a bully boss and they are unable to escape this misery, it means that they are in a very desperate situation. When I had to work under a bully boss, I started to feel that I cannot even work in the same industry as the boss. I am a very passionate, career-oriented woman, but working under this bully boss made

me insane. I used to question why I had to come this far in my career. Sometimes, we have to work under a bully boss because they pay our bills. I cannot advise people to leave their jobs without putting together a better plan. Staying in this misery is as difficult as leaving it and becoming homeless. That is why this part is the most difficult one. Let me try helping you with my long, exhausting journey.

When I was working under a bully boss, I don't know if I made her life miserable or she made mine. I remember her being demoted after I left, but the thing which disturbed the most is that my immediate boss created this complicated situation and even the boss's boss fell for it. I would definitely recommend having a good relationship with your boss, because if it turns complicated, the next step is either you have to leave or you burn in this hell. You have to remember that technically every resource is dispensable. This is not a loving or caring relationship where you will try to make things work after you have developed a bad taste in your mouth. In this bad experience, only one person survives; the other person leaves. I had to leave in my case and all I remember is the physical and emotional trauma I had to handle. My heart would stop (rhetorically) with an e-mail notification on my phone. I would pray that it is not another work issue that she had prepared for me. I used to break down emotionally several times, but I tried my best to keep it all together. If she brought up an issue, I would have had all the evidence ready to support me. It was exhausting. The workplace became like a war space. This was not why I had come so far in my professional life. I never knew how it feels to work under someone who doesn't want you to progress. When I joined, I heard a lot about how she had ruined so many professional lives in her department. I had full sympathy for her. Being a strong believer in kindness, I met her with a neutral attitude and was willing to give her my support. She had amazing administrative skills, her paperwork was perfect, her files were extraordinary, but I don't know what happened to her people skills. I don't know a single person in our department who was not a victim of her bullying behaviour. My actual issue started over my annual appraisal. I rejected it and requested for a review. I challenged her decision and this was when she showed me her worst side. She created false scenarios to ruin my reputation. I had to dig out previous e-mails and messages to support my case. Can you imagine how hard it was to look at the good side of life at that time?

My career is very important to me. Getting this far in my career was not easy. Let me share a little background on my career struggle. Coming from a conservative family, I didn't have many options to pursue my dreams. You will know more about this story.

Before I got married, my father-in-law passed away. My husband had to support his family for some time. We did not have a lot of money to spend, so I started to work. I enjoyed office and the working environment. I wanted to achieve a lot in my career. In Asian families, it is a common norm to force a couple right after marriage to have a child. My first daughter was the result of this pressure. My mother-in-law was very supportive in raising our kids, so I continued my work. After my daughter was born, our financial situation improved. Apparently, it was ok if I didn't work anymore, but now I was enjoying my identity and the acknowledgement I got from work. Maybe since family members don't acknowledge each other, my capabilities being recognised at work was a good feeling. I kept working on my career. I loved hearing the words "working mother." After my maternity leave, I went back to work. My daughter's tiny existence used to control my ambitions. I started my Master's while working and conceived my second child. With this amazing company, I completed my Master's and I had my second child. When my second child turned two, my husband was transferred to Dubai. My promotion was due in a few months and I was tempted to get the new title. Now I was confused about whether I should go with him or stay back in Pakistan for some time. It was hard for me to decide. I realised that in this culture only one person can have a full-fledged career; the other party will have to adjust for the kids. So I resigned from my job and moved with him to Dubai. It took us a few months to settle in, and as soon as my kids started to go to school, I started to look for a job. I was looking for part-time options since I didn't have anyone to look after my kids at this point. My first financial engagement didn't pay me much. I used to go for two hours and my compensation was just enough to pay for my taxi fare. After doing similar small assignments, I got a proper job with amazing financial compensation. This is where I got my dream job with my not-so-dream boss. I was in this job for five years.

I feel I went against the odds to keep my career. I worked so hard for a decent career and now, with the bully boss, everything was going down the drain. I just couldn't take the ill-treatment at work. How could I let my boss undermine my skills after I had worked so hard? With all this going on, I got pregnant again. Somehow, I succumbed to the emotional pressure to have a third child. This time, my kids and my husband were the reason. This pregnancy was by choice and our kids were our motivation to go through this process again. I was pregnant and at the mercy of my bully boss. Anyways, it was Allah's will, and we couldn't meet our third child alive. This pregnancy was complicated from the beginning, and I was under a lot of stress from my boss. We were in a kind of war-like situation and eventually she won. I had to leave the job and I lost my child on my way out. I will not blame anyone, but it was not easy. I went into early labour and I delivered a stillborn in my bathroom. I lost a fully formed baby. I had never felt so helpless in my life. For the first time, I realised how "losing" someone feels like. I realised that however much you try, if something is not meant to be, it is not meant to be. That day I realised how helpless I was in reality. No matter how much I wanted something, I couldn't have it. This was the first wake-up call to my ego and stubbornness. My powerlessness made me humble. My perspective on controlling things changed. This emotional setback put me in a place where I turned numb towards my bully boss. As I mentioned earlier, I had rejected my performance evaluation, which created a lot of complications. It got so complicated that my boss's boss had to come in. After my miscarriage, they moved me to another department and I started to report to another person. Now this new person was my boss and, gosh, how relieved I was! It was an amazing workplace though. Great people, superb systems and environment. Except for my immediate boss, everything was good. Unfortunately, I could not stay there for long. I made a few mistakes on that job and I regret it. Anyways, I completed my contract and I promised myself that I would not work under any boss ever again. I wasn't sure if I could handle this trauma again. I wanted to work but I wasn't ready to work under anyone. I decided to get my own license and I started to work as a freelancer. My personality is not as outgoing as a salesperson or a business development person's should be, but I was willing to do anything except accepting a boss in my life again. I put myself out there and I was out of my comfort zone. I had always worked under someone and now being on my own needed another mindset.

I worked as a freelancer for one year. I started my business as a soft skills specialist. I would train people on people management skills so that they don't torture other people around them. I am sure you know where this inspiration came from. If you have a boss who bullies, kindly ask them to join my training program. On the other hand, if you are a boss who bullies other people, I am sure you don't realise that you have to be a bit kind. You wouldn't know how much damage you are causing to other people and how it's taking you away from your organisational goals as well. I know a bully boss can find it very difficult to see the big picture, but this bully model is not sustainable in the long run and in one way or another, it hurts everyone. Kindly feel free to drop me an e-mail to get a customised program for yourself. ☺

During this time, one of my old employers approached me. They had opened a training institute in Dubai and they wanted me to manage it. Now with this offer, I was both happy and nervous. Happy because I would have a structure to work again and nervous because I have to work under a boss again. I was confused, but I wanted to give this situation a 2nd chance. I started a conversation with my mind on finding any evidence that this boss would be as bad as the one before. I couldn't find any evidence since I had not worked under this gentleman before. Me being the biggest advocate of how I should see beyond my irritations and try giving this opportunity a chance, I signed up for the job. I stayed in this job for a year and a half and, trust me, this was the best boss I ever had. I was happy that I gave myself another chance to work under someone. I got tremendous exposure in a leadership position. I was very happy that I didn't go with my mind's initial decision.

Self-talk:
Would avoiding work opportunities help you? No, it will not. Will you be happy if you don't try this new work option? I am not sure at the moment. If you are not sure, then how are you making this decision?

I don't know. I want to try but I am scared. What are you scared of? I am scared if this boss will be as terrible as the last one. Ok, what are the chances that he is a bully like your last boss? I don't know. Well, if you don't know then how are you deciding? Well, yeah, it is complicated. Ok, suppose this boss is not like the one before, how do you feel now, and if you don't take this opportunity, what will you lose now? Well, I will lose this leadership experience and I will lose a schedule and regular monthly income. So how do you feel about it? I feel like my goal is greater than my worry. I would like this leadership experience, this regular income and a schedule. I am tempted to try out this position and in case my boss is a bully, just in case, I will leave the job early this time. Ok, this seems to be a reasonable decision. Yes, it does.

So this is how self-talk helps in clearing the mental cloud. This is where I didn't give a chance to my bully boss but I was able to trust another person in the same position. It is ok if you become part of the same scene with new characters. You will agree with me that everyone is not the same. I know it's difficult to trust your decision-making skills and capabilities once they are emotionally crushed, but it is important to regain confidence in your decision-making skills.

Reflection chair:
Example:
What will I lose if I don't take this offer? (Answer: I will lose trust in my capabilities.) Will all my efforts for my career go down the drain? Is this end of my career? Will I

be happy if I don't get this experience? How will I know about this experience if I don't try?

Flip: New Thoughts and Feelings

It's your turn. Add your notes here!

6

2ND CHANCE TO YOURSELF

I belong to a conservative family from Pakistan. We were three sisters, and my parents desperately wanted a boy. When I was born, my mother wanted to give me to my aunt and my father took the decision to keep me. My mum tells me that at first she was very annoyed at my birth since I was a girl, but when she held me her world changed, and to date I am her favourite daughter. As we grew up, my parents were extremely keen on us getting married. In our culture, it's a big thing that girls should be married at a certain age. So, since my parents had been keenly pursuing it, all three of us got married at the "perfect age." Well, almost perfect! ☺

Financially, my parents were a middle-class family so spending on education was not a priority but, yes, spending on weddings was appreciated. It's again a cultural thing and the girl's parents are under a lot of pressure in Asian culture when their daughters are married. In fact, in my culture, a daughter's birth is seen as a burden and a boy's birth is celebrated. Though in my religion, it's totally the opposite, but since we are historically influenced, we have few cultural pain points. I was not happy with so many things in our culture that I developed a defence mechanism of being stubborn. I got so irritated at times that I would even break crockery when angered. God bless my parents for being patient with me.

So, finally I got married and I started to work. My parents were not very happy in the beginning. They used to tell me to quit work and take care of the family. At one point of time, my mother-in-law also wanted the same. This used to irritate me a lot. I used to think I am working so hard to have a career and kids, so why was everyone against it? My rebellious nature kept me going. Luckily, my company was amazing and I felt appreciated and motivated to work. I worked there for nine years, until my husband was asked to relocate to Dubai.

After moving to Dubai, you know about my bully boss experience and my miscarriage. These two things were enough to traumatise me, and I was dependent on my husband for emotional support. Within two months of these unfortunate events, I found out that my husband is not what I thought he was. I discovered questionable messages on his phone. He would say, "It doesn't mean anything," but I will call it flirting or cheating.

I would like to add another thing here—that my husband is aware of this content. We are willingly sharing this pain so that you can learn from our experience. My husband and I went through a difficult patch. In my eyes, what he did was a big hit to my values and my existence. The reason to share this information is so that you see how people outgrow mishaps. If you are going through the same, maybe this book can give you some insights on how to steer your energy. After this incident, I became very serious about myself. Instead of leaving the situation and being miserable, I managed to outdo myself. I gave myself another chance. I had two choices—to disappear and leave everything or stay and fight my demons. I chose the latter. That was the darkest time in our relationship. It still creates trouble sometimes; it still haunts me but I try to practice all the NLP (Neuro-Linguistic Programming), CBT (Cognitive Behaviour Therapy), and EQ (Emotional Quotient) tools to keep me grounded.

My biggest tragedy was this situation with my husband, but yet again, this gave the most strength to love myself. People used to think I was depressed due to the miscarriage and everyone used to say that it's ok since I had two more kids. I couldn't share this with anyone until now. This was the biggest reason why I sought professional help. I went to a psychiatrist and clinical psychologist. I took medicines and CBT treatment for six months. I asked my husband to leave me. He clearly disapproved of this idea and he convinced me to make a fresh start. In the next few months, he truly attempted to change the situation. I will give myself the credit for not making any rash decision about our marriage and I will give him credit for not giving up on us. You can call me weak or a scary loser or someone who compromised on values, but I think giving this marriage a 2nd chance was one of the best decisions I have made. Mentally and morally, I am not the same any more. I think I have compromised on my values because of my kids and parents. But this story has another angle to it. I realised that I can achieve more if I stay in this marriage instead of starting from scratch. I am not kidding when I say that I have grown from this experience and have put it behind me. I have truly given myself another chance. It was not easy at that time. This mishap gave me a new perspective. I became more confident and strong. Now, after losing everything, I just wanted to be at peace. I shared this incident with a few close friends and you will be surprised to know that they too are living with almost the same pain. I don't know if it's a generational thing, situational thing, or something else. If you are in a situation like this, divert all your energies to develop yourself instead of blaming someone and feeling miserable. In my culture, it is easy to stay married and work on yourself instead of leaving everything and being lost. I didn't have any other problems in my marriage. My emotional needs are still not met but I think it doesn't bother me anymore. I have found solace in my work, kids, and friends. Staying in a marriage is not an option if you have an abusive husband or someone who denies your existence. In that case, your model of giving yourself a chance will be different from mine. Just tell yourself that *you* are "now your priority." How will you take care of yourself, where will you flourish more? You need a conducive environment to grow. Explore insights, talk to yourself, investigate options, see where you are less miserable, and then go for that option. In my case, I know I am better off with my husband instead of leaving him. I just had to rearrange a few things in my marriage.

This feeling of being taken advantage of, rejected, humiliated, and hurt was very new to me. I couldn't process so many emotions at that time or understand what the right decision was. I needed time. I couldn't take my life's biggest decision under the spell of negativity. I wanted time to process and understand the current situation, its consequences, and everything else. It took me so much time to gain clarity that the incident became history. I know it is complicated and I have no words to justify whatever happened and why it happened. I just feel that giving another chance to this relationship was very important. Our religion says that, in some circumstances, if you suffer in a situation, there is a possibility that nature wants to guide someone. It is not about you; you are just a channel to someone else's maturity or benefit. So does it mean that I had to find this out so my husband can stop doing this? Well I do not know, but it is not a bad belief to keep, especially if it helps me understand why I had to know what I know. It is very hard to stay with people who hurt you and damage your existence. I did that . . . and I don't regret it.

After I got out of my reflection, I knew my priorities. I became fearless. I remember being rebellious again. This wrong made everything right in my life. I flipped, same coin but a different side. I turned this irritation into opportunity. I worked on my self like never before. This book is also a result of that journey. I know now that I am my priority. I told you the two prerequisites to 2nd chances:

1. Passion.
2. Healing.

In my case, I had passion but now I had to heal before I could move on with my life. I started practicing self-love like never before. I went for CBT and that was the best decision in my life. CBT and NLP changed my life. These two schools of thought share so much wisdom about individual behaviour that it can change your life. You can imagine that, in today's world, being emotionally kind to each other is very rare. We are very harsh towards other people's mistakes. We are not very forgiving. After any emotional trauma, it is important that we practice healing. We should fix the damaged road before we can ride our car on it. The damaged road (our inner self) will only hurt us.

In case you are wondering, my husband and I are doing well. We went to couple therapy. I am a new me, and the rest is history.

Self-talk:
I cannot live with this humiliation. I feel terrible. These are only chat messages. Why are you taking it so hard on yourself? But for me, even these messages are too much and, honestly, I don't know what else would have happened. I don't know. I am just hurt and I don't know what to do. Ok, ask yourself—what will you get if you leave him? Oh, I will be miserable.

2ND CHANCE TO YOURSELF 59

I cannot imagine myself without him and plus, society will not accept me as a single woman. I have kids and their future will be at stake. I don't earn like before so I am not sure how I will support myself financially. Ok, how do you feel miserable living without him? I feel miserable living with him but I think this misery will be less than what I will experience if I leave him. Ok, let's see what my religion has to say on this. My religion says believe in Allah, forgive one time, and make a fresh start.

Reflection chair:

What is this experience teaching me? How can I make things different for myself? Does this mean that I have to revisit who I should spend my time on? What do I need to do now? Do I have the resources to understand this situation clearly? Can I change my priorities? Does this mean that I should work on myself more than anything else? What did I gain out of this experience?

Flip: New Thoughts and Feelings

It's your turn now. Add your notes here!

7

MINDSET MATTERS

Soft Skills Model
If you want to improve your interpersonal skills, you have to work on your intrapersonal skills. I am a soft skills specialist and mentor by profession. I work with many clients and companies to improve and refresh their people management skills. Following this simple model will give mind-blowing results.

Soft skills are all those skills which you need to manage yourself and other people. It includes communication, adaptability, EQ, leadership, etc. All these skills are equally important and they are used in a different capacity, depending on the situation. If you want to know more about soft skills you can Google and it will give you an extensive list of all the skills.

I will share what worked with my clients. I am sure this is universal knowledge and this chapter is a mere reminder of that. If you want to work on your soft skills, you have to first work on your mindset, then emotions, and last you have to work on improving your soft skills (Figure as under).

In fact, all this happens very smoothly together. To have a lasting impact, you have to work on your belief and mindset. You can listen to millions of lectures and vid Belief), your building will be very weak. I will just give you an idea of this model. Next to mindset, emotions, and soft skills, you can add as many related pointers as you want to.

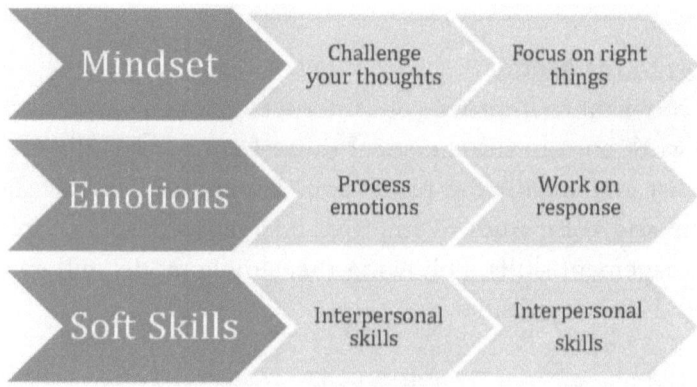

ST Soft Skills Model

At current times, we have all the information. Researchers are doing extraordinary work. Gaining knowledge is not a problem. If you want any information, you scan/search the Internet and you have it all available. The problem is that, we know what to do and we are still not doing it. Application, action, and practice are an issue. Our action becomes easy if our mindset is aligned to our goals. This takes practice. Anything you want to work on, it all starts with your mindset. We have to grow from our experiences.

The setbacks are never-ending. ☺ Growing up, I used to stutter until the age of fifteen. If you meet me now, you wouldn't even realise that I'd had a speech issue. I recovered from stuttering just with my mind. I changed many mental models so that my stuttering doesn't come in my way. The mind is an interesting thing. I was interested to know how our brain and emotions work. I came across a book, *How Emotions Are Made* by Lisa Feldman Barrett. It says that our brain, trapped in a skull, is always busy and is predicting the outside world based on our past experiences as a guide.

I feel that we are always fighting with our mind. Technically, it is a small part of our body but it controls everything. It's important that it does the job it is supposed to do, but somehow I feel it doesn't guide us right all the time. A small part of our body, always closeted in the dark, relies on signals from our eyes, nose, ears, etc.—working on a preprogrammed structure, usually based on experiences. How much should we rely on its presumed structures?

Let's pause for a bit. The brain in the skull—visualise this picture in your mind. Apparently, it is a very dark place to be in. If something is in a dark place, what do we expect from it? After being proven wrong, shaken up to the core, I understood that I cannot trust my mind blindly. It will rely on past experiences mostly. What can I do to think otherwise?

This made me think that, truly, when people are kind to a kid, that kid also turns out to be kind and vice versa, but if someone is not kind to you, you pass on this behaviour to ten more people, based on how they communicated or how they looked or how they made you feel? We get so stubborn when it comes to judging people that we work towards building walls instead of being comfortable in one space.

In all the situations of my life that I've described, whatever decision I took was based on my mindset and feelings. I know something that helped me was asking questions to myself; all sorts of questions. When we ask questions, we find a balance between our rational mind and emotional mind. The lord has given us an accelerator for emotions and a brake for questions to drive this car without hurting anyone or ourselves. In this chapter, we will explore a hypothetical situation in more details. You can imagine that you have disapproved an option.

Ask yourself why you disapproved this option.
Did it not meet your values?

If not, how harmful is it to be flexible with your values?

Are these values greater than your bigger goal in life?

With time, can you change the situation as per your values?

Did you reject that option because of the person on the other side of the table?

What bothered you most about that person?

How much interaction is needed with that particular person?

What is more important? Your ultimate goal or that person?

Reevaluate your mood.

Is there something else bothering you?

What is the worst that will happen if you reconsider the option you rejected?

What solid evidence do you have that your assumption about this rejected option is true?

Such reaffirmations and challenging questions will give you deep insights. I come from a collectivist society, and I know how damaging it is to keep carrying other people's emotional baggage with us. We don't question anything, we don't challenge any ill feeling, and we fall for cognitive biases. We South Asians stay FOREVER within families; and when so many people are interacting on a regular basis, it is very natural to fall for any irrelevant drama. Living with a huge family has its benefits, but we have to understand that too many utensils in one cupboard will make noise. (This is a popular Urdu proverb.)

Problems begin when we start depending on these people for our emotional needs. If someone does not meet our expectation, we try to find an ally. We will talk about (b**ch) that person to other people and we will try to find some emotional support. People rely on other people's feedback instead of developing a personal opinion. For example, if my close family member is not happy with me, he/she will conspire to get a whole crew against me. They will try to find people who can endorse their judgment. Those who don't know me better will fall for this trap. Eventually, it gets so dirty that you actually start acting like the bad apple in the family.

I have seen this happen to many families. In a collectivist society, sometimes everyone's only entertainment is to talk about other people. We associate ourselves with the people around us; we want to be accepted and belong. This feeling of wanting to "belong" is good but if it is developed at the cost of hurting others, it is not worth it. Our mind likes excitement, and being in a big family, gossip is the easiest way to get that excitement. It is ironic that we try to create complications in other people's relationships and then we expect that those relationships should not be broken at any cost. In South Asia, a husband or wife leaving each other or grown-up kids leaving their parents is a big deal. It is not easily accepted or appreciated. So it is like they will make you hate each other and yet, you cannot leave the relationship. How sad is this?

In my family, I am known to be a very neutral person whenever there is an issue. I don't agree to be part of any drama if I don't have complete information from both the parties. I only play the role of a spectator and do not add any opinions. Let me remind you again, I think my passion played a very important role in keeping me away from all the unnecessary dramas.

Let us ask some questions:
When you are irritated, do you share your irritation with other people?

Do you enjoy it when the same person is discussed in a negative way by a third party? Have you ever stopped them?

What do you think will happen if you don't take other people with you on your hate trip?

We have one more trait in general as human beings—we are brutally honest when we have to share something negative about someone, and these "honest police" identify themselves as being true to heart. They will be very proud that they don't indulge in any drama and that is why people don't like them. I know some people, who are close to me, do this. I ask them why sharing negative things is the only honesty we practice. If someone sees actual goodness in another person and they cherish this truly, why can't that be taken as honesty? Well, growing up, I have always been scolded for asking these questions and I never got an answer. I understand we have to make an effort to look for goodness in life, but how long before we start practicing it?

Our mind has a natural inclination towards what is wrong, and yet we feed our mind by focusing on what is incorrect because we feel challenged and we think that we are solving a problem. By cutting off people around you, without a moment of reflection or without learning anything from these experiences, you are not solving your problems; you are actually adding to them.

Question time:
How can you make things better for yourself?

What can you do alternatively instead of cutting people from your life?

To answer so many thought-provoking questions, let me give you some direction on how to steer your thinking boat:

1. Don't assume you know everything about the other person.
2. Understand that everyone is different from each other.
3. You being right doesn't mean that the other person is wrong and vice versa.
4. Have goals which are bigger than your social interactions.
5. You can kindly and courteously minimise your interaction with the person who annoys you.
6. Do yourself a favour and don't share your irritation with a third person. When people irritate us, we love to discuss it with other people. Notice a pattern.

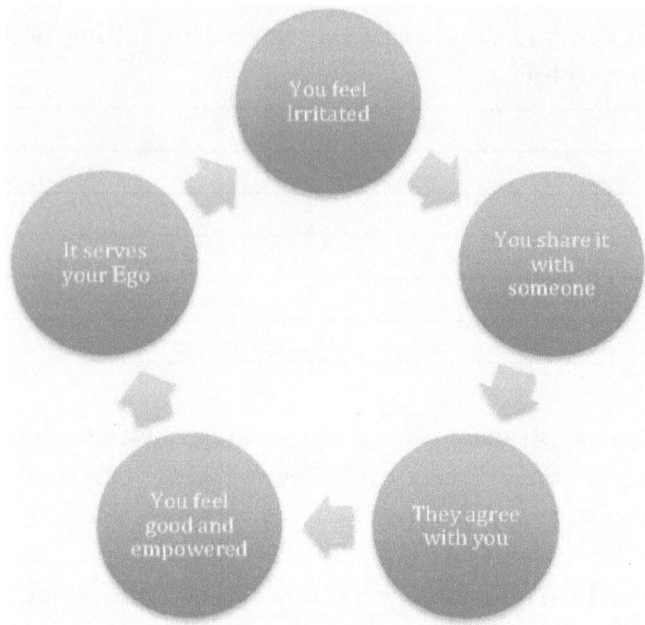

Irritation serving the Ego

In the above picture, it illustrates how, when you feel irritated, you share it with someone, they agree with you, you feel good and empowered, it serves your ego, and you repeat the same cycle just for that ego-boosting feeling of being right. Next time, if you are tempted to do so, just think about whether it is helping you achieve your life goals. If you don't have a life goal, then you can enjoy this circle, but not having any goal is another sad part of life. However, strategies to identify life goals are not part of this book, but then again, maybe it's just another point to find answers.

Going back to the diagram, do you find yourself stuck in this loop of "Irritation serving the Ego" or talking about people and getting that adrenaline rush of being right?

Let me ask you a question.

How about if you don't share your bad experience?

Someone might say, "We need to tell other people so I can save them."

(Well, you are making someone else drown in this case.)

Reflection time:

My next challenging thought is:

- Maybe you are the only person he/she irritates.
- Maybe you were in a bad mood and that's why you are offended.
- Maybe your expectations are not met somehow.
- Maybe that person has different ways of processing information and how they behave.

Ask yourself some honest questions:

How stubborn or flexible are you in your thinking?

How patient are you with other people?

Have you ever been treated badly by someone in your life?

How did it affect you?

Who did you blame when you were not treated right?

Who do you blame now if you don't treat someone right?

Are you uncomfortable around people who don't align with your thought process?

How do you escape situations you are not comfortable in?

I am sure many a times you might have had bad experiences with someone in life. Ask yourself:

How often are you irritated?

How often do you share your experience with a third party?

Will you be able to break this "Irritation serving the Ego" loop? And how?

8

"SOMETIMES BUILDING A NEW BRIDGE IS A LOT OF WORK COMPARED TO FIXING THE OLD ONE"

When we have a tough life, it can be difficult to be kind to others. I know a few people in my surroundings. They don't trust the system. They are angry at Mother Nature. Some of them make jokes that are meant to hurt other people. I don't know what sort of mindset this is, but I do know that it causes a lot of damage internally. I am not saying that I have recovered from all the damage I experienced, but I know one thing for sure—that I can handle it in a better way now. My problems and scars are not very obvious. I love my family and that is why I heal myself everyday so I don't hurt anyone.

I want to have a little more discussion on relationships with our spouse or family. I understand that sometimes we don't have a choice when it comes to our family, but is it that easy to close all the doors and build walls around us with our ignorance and arrogance? The problem in my part of the world is that even if people are miserable in a relationship, they would prefer not to talk about it or fix it. We have huge communication and understanding issues and we assume that the other party should know what we want, without saying it. We carry years of emotional baggage, and no one is willing to drop it. In fact, we have a few bags kept for the worst situations. These bags come out with a lot of hate at the wrong times, and create another bag of emotional turmoil, which is good to be carried for a few more days, until it changes into something more stupid. In our culture, most marriages sustain due to family pressure, either from parents or kids. This is sad to see—that hearts and minds don't connect and you still live in the same house like so-called partners. I have seen one more trend in homes—partners are very nice and happy outside, but as soon as they enter their house they become warriors; like they are at war with someone inside the house. They will barely smile or talk and they will focus on what is wrong instead of what is right. I know these three people in my family; everybody loves them. They are available for everyone. They are very witty and kind. People think that their family is so lucky. On the other hand, since I have seen them in their homes, I know how emotionally closed and negative they are around their families. I could never understand this attitude.

- Why are some people so irritated around their own families?
- Why do some people prefer not to fix issues within their family?

This is very sad, and I don't know how relationships can be healthy in such a scenario. Mostly, relationships are transactional; partners find some sort of benefits to stay together or they try to avoid any trouble that comes their way. The story is going another way, but do you see a connection? The connection is that we are conditioned to make things work for better or for worse. This conditioning can be a strength if we use it wisely. If we are married, we try to give ourselves reasons to fall in love with the same person again and again. This is how I got the courage to apply this mindset to the outside world and try giving people, situations, and myself 2nd chances. I feel very light when I know that I am not carrying anyone else's burden and that I am not passing on any burden. It is truly liberating. Sometimes, your purpose becomes bigger. In my case, purpose has given me the power to stay grounded. I choose between people or purpose. When my purpose is big, the people around me don't bother me.

I was listening to this spiritual scholar and a point he made just stuck with me. Imagine how we take care of our garden and plants, so that they can grow well and give us flowers, fruits, or vegetables. Every plant needs a different setting. How about if we look at our relationships as gardens? In order to get a good garden, we have to pour in a generous amount of soil and the right amount of sunlight and water. It is the same with relationships; they need generous amounts of love, respect, and care if we want to enjoy the fruit, otherwise the plant (relationship) will die. Yes, we do get some termites and dead bushes sometimes; we have to remove them, otherwise they will damage our garden. Similarly, in relationships, we have to treat negative thinking and prejudice (bushes and insects), otherwise our whole garden will be ruined. How beautiful is this analogy?

Let us take this analogy further:
What bushes and termites do you find in your relationship?

If you had the power to remove it, what would you do?

What resources do you need for this?

What would you say to yourself and your partner if I tell you that those bushes and termites come naturally, that it is no one's fault?

Our mind is naturally inclined towards negativity; if we let it do what it wants, we will get the same results over and over again. We will usually get the same results if it is processed in the same way all the time. To explore options, we should expand experience and dialogue. Self-talk is the enlightenment that you need. Don't shy away from talking to yourself; even at the scariest moments, try to have a conversation with yourself like a boss—have conversations that will solve your problems. Make sure you advocate a positive scenario, even if you don't feel like it. Don't be overwhelmed with positivity. However, you have to have a balance. Tell yourself that you don't want negative thoughts and you don't want to indulge in "daydreaming." Finding a balance between positive thoughts and negative thoughts is the key. I feel this strategy has worked the best for me. You will be surprised that I used to get scared when things would go right. I would think it is too much, that I cannot be happy since something "bad" is just around the corner, that "bad" will see that I am happy and will show itself and I will become sad. So I would pretend not to be so happy so the bad wouldn't come. I guess you can relate to this. Sometimes, we are so scared when something good has happened that we wait, thinking that it will definitely be followed by something bad.

I have had many negative thoughts on several occasions. The mind loves negative thoughts; positive thoughts don't come to us naturally. I had to work on it, and my CBT treatment gave me that strength and my NLP made me more aware on how I should manage myself and others. CBT taught me to challenge my thoughts and ask for evidence when I feared something. I started to have a productive dialogue with my mind. Honestly now, whenever I am going into a negative mindset, I literally get into a dialogue with my mind. I ask questions for clarity. When my mind is not clear with the answers, I explore, by giving my rejected options a chance. I tell myself that I want to be doubly sure before I reject any option.

If you are confused in your interaction with someone, try filling out these boxes.

Why should I meet that person?

Why am I not comfortable with this person?

Have I ever had any experience with this person before? If yes, how bad was it?

What are the pros and cons of this interaction?

How much is at stake?

SOMETIMES BUILDING A NEW BRIDGE IS A LOT OF WORK

Why do I need to explore options?

Why should I take this risk?

Why should I bother exploring options like that?

Why do we associate so much like and dislike towards people?

Can we put people in neutral boxes?

How hard is it to not passionately hate or love someone?

Is it possible to keep most people in a grey area and focus on your life goals?

9

CONCLUSION

Treat this book as your diary. No one needs to know the answers. You can be honest and true to yourself. Don't bring in ego while answering the questions. These answers will release the emotional baggage that you have been carrying. Of course, if you are enjoying the baggage, you are more than welcome to carry it. When you are ready to transition to your higher self, you can always refer to this book. These exercises will give you the liberty to be your true self. This is the time to grow up and set yourself free from all those messed-up relationships and circumstances you experienced. Reflect on all the experiences, learn from them, Flip and become a better version of yourself.

Sadly, I know someone who doesn't believe in the goodness of the world. Whenever you try to tell them anything nice, their reply is, "Yeah, I know everything," or "You don't know how I feel; you haven't been in my position." My heart agrees since I know they have seen tough times, but my mind says that they can do better. I know for a fact that this person is so negative towards life that it is becoming toxic for most of the people around them. Good days are ok for them, but bad days are like hell. Surviving through bad days is not easy, but the damage we do on those days becomes irreversible. If you don't want to live big dreams, kindly don't create chaos on bad days. Bad days will only define your life if you let them. Who doesn't have a tough life? Ok, if you think you are more miserable when compared to everyone else, then you should have been the one working more on leaving all that emotional baggage.

If this wakes up anything in you, maybe you can start healing now so you don't waste the rest of your life. You know, there is one more sad aspect of toxicity. We had a rough day, and we treated someone very badly, and, unfortunately, this happened more than once. Now you have realised, over time, that what you did was wrong, but the other person will not forget it. It will come back to you in a different scenario. It is like that ocean wave with a barrier; it will come back stronger every time. The more irritated we are with others, the more irritation we receive. We have been told to not go on roads we closed, not to talk to people we dislike, not to fix things that are not working. I think we dislike very passionately and we waste our energy in being judgmental even when it is not needed.

CONCLUSION

Everyone talks about walking away. How about if we just stay and try to understand the true scenario? Remember, to stay, you have to heal first. To heal yourself, you need to find help. To find help, you have to realise that it still hurts. If it hurts, it hurts—there is no third option. Hurting all the time is exhausting. I am sure you will realise this once you are truly ready to heal yourself. Find your passion and be less judgmental about the people around you.

We all have our experiences; learning from those experiences is where the magic is. You are stronger than your problems and you have every right to be loved and others also deserve to be loved. Let us try; the hate can go away without leaving scars. Let care and love be the new cool.

Sending lots of love to all my readers.

DISCLAIMER

The examples given are true, personal stories. While narrating them, if by mistake I have used anyone else's analogy or theory, kindly let me know so I can give due credit. With so much repetitive material out there, it is hard to keep track. I hope you will understand.

www.ingramcontent.com/pod-product-compliance
Lightning Source LLC
Chambersburg PA
CBHW021157080526
44588CB00008B/377

9 781922 456120